Alun, a
oddwel
mebefsm 7013.

Cowlfon, Clcheldre 'Coerijbri'
Clbb

EQUALIZING THE DAY

EQUALIZING
THE DAY

CHAS PARRY-JONES

HEADLAND

First published in 2013 by
Headland Publications
Tŷ Coch, Galltegfa,
Llanfwrog, Ruthin,
Denbighshire LL15 2AR

ISBN 978 1 902096 13 1
Copyright © 2013 Chas Parry-Jones

Printed in Great Britain by
Oriel Studios, Orrell Mount
Hawthorne Road, Merseyside L20 6NS

To my dear wife Helen who introduced me to opera and classical music, but significantly awakened me to the meaning of life.

ACKNOWLEDGEMENTS

Thanks are due to the editors of the following publications, magazines and anthologies, where some of these poems have previously appeared:

Yr Arwydd, Ynys Mon Papur bro with translations into Welsh by Glyndwr Thomas; *Anglesey Anthology,* editor Dewi Roberts; *Basics Journal; Country Quest* 1969 to 1975; *The Listening Shell, Tŷ Newydd,* editor Gladys Mary Coles; *Poetry Wales,* Editor Zoë Skoulding; *Medical News; Montage,* editor Edwina Jones; *Rural Wales* CPRW; *The Roundyhouse,* editor Sally Roberts Jones; *Skald,* Editor Zoë Skoulding; *North Wales Review; Quattrocento,* editor Malcolm Bradbury; *Talwrn Archaeological Newsletter,* editor Ann Benwell.

My thanks to Professor John Bailey, University of Oxford, widower of Dame Iris Murdoch for his kind words and encouragement.
Gladys Mary Coles of the University of Liverpool for her praise and stimulation.

The painting on the cover is by William Parry-Jones MA Fine Art, Cardiff

My thanks to Dr Edward Parry-Jones for his computer knowledge and valuable aid, and to my daughter Charlotte Jones Davies for her belief in the project.

CONTENTS

The Mail Boat	9
Coombe Ambulance	10
Halloween	11
Autumnal Equinox Michaelmas	12
Equalizing the Day	13
Shaving Jug	14
Kyffin	15
The Stable	16
Sun Worship	17
The Old Boat	17
Anglesey Mist	18
Red Wharf Bay	18
News on the Half Hour	19
Learning the Gaelic	20
Valentine Card	21
Gorse Blossom	21
Cwm Pennant Picnic	22
Good Friday	22
Dic	24
Collecting the Eggs	26
Capel Moriah	27
Melin Eithin	28
Bus to Market	29
Brindle Dog	30
Letter to Iris Murdoch	31
Bryan	32
Mozart String Quartet	33
The Tank, Benllech	34
Drowning in Music	35
Keep Your Bloody Chips Deiniolen	36
Macleod and I	37
Medical Housing Pointing in Dolgellau	38
Fearful Silence	39
Gladiators	40
La Gioconda	41

CONTENTS (continued)

Gwerclas	42
Flint Castle	44
Pair Walking	45
Walking in Pairs	46
What's on the Pictures?	47
Home from the Plaza	48
The Rape of the Stair	49
Irish Washerwoman	51
The Old Convent	52
Jane Welsh Carlyle	53
Hunting the Wren	55
Asleep	56
New Lips	57
International Smiles	58
Renoir's Garden	58
Tŷ Newydd, Winter 1945	59
Lon Penmynedd	60
Siwan's Farewell	62
Henffordd Abergwyngregin	63
Pandy Benllech	64
Pilgrimage	65
Bluebottle	66
Morning Epiphany	67
My Head	68
Waiting Room	68
Biographical Note	70

THE MAIL BOAT

Railways and ships have vapours
Of the night train newspapers,
Steam gone,
Fish-clear cold faced air
Freshens my moist eyes,
Which stare
Into the dark at the rail
For the slow shape of the mail.
The station fills her stable,
Two ships linked by a cable,
Their bows
From the dock climbing,
Limpid green water lapping,
Hibernia and *Cambria*,
They were never in closer,
As in Holyhead harbour
In love at the midnight hour.

COOMBE AMBULANCE (in 1959)

The children some barefoot come running
moths collecting round a white ambulance
on the corner of that street
where the Grand Canal lies
cool and dark over the railings

one girl says to her pal
Janey! 'tis' n amblance!
Hold your collar 'till we see a dog!
Oi'll look afther it Mistha!
says another boy, the leader
Mistha 0i'll keep 'em off for sixpence!

I once left a girl in labour
in Inchicore, the flats,
to find all my tyres let down
standing by the very same
Heinz bean tin and *Evening Herald*
I had remembered two weeks before
by the bicycle wheel in the gutter.

I wish we had them things they say
you can get from over the water
says the twenty one year old mother of five,
the Coombe ambulance was safe,
her baby born alive and healthy,
another mouth to feed
and receive all Dublin could supply.

HALLOWEEN

I recognize this feeling of excitement tonight
remember it as a child and later as a youngster
the same height of the sun in the early evening
through the trees
when setting off for a dance
being at the junction of the seasons
weather systems above
diverging clouds streaming
the wind changing direction
birds flying about in a disturbed way
rabbits creeping down from the wood
and a hedgehog on the lawn
the air is yet warm and a little humid
the year on the brink of adulthood.

But no one ever said anything
it was not remarked upon.
The sunlight was somewhat whiter
the brown night still full embracing and friendly
as we came out of the sweating dancehall
in sequence
walking home in pairs and groups
after the last bus
strolling along musical pavements.
I look now at Helen walking up to the butchers,
and then she is gone
in the haze of the buddleia at the gate.

AUTUMN EQUINOX, MICHAELMAS

Today is the day
sunrise is to be due East
since day and night are equal
sunset will be due West
space time continuum
somewhere in between

string running out
over our ash tree
spun beyond
to the Irish sea
salty wet neutrons
electrons and quarks
spots winking in and out
sparks blinking
but
our daisies are blooming now in August
a month before they should
though Michael's boss and all the Archangels
try as hard as they could
Piano! Piano! Piano! he calls
in his best Italianate Vatican
but it's all that he can
do against a future
that is so sure
that nothing should stay the same
when climate change
is the name of the game.

EQUALIZING THE DAY

An alfresco moment
as innocent
as a rare bird seen,
unaware of her significance,
equalizes the day for me,
vanishes disability
amazingly,
and makes a bond.
God is the truth of which
goodness is the reality.

SHAVING JUG

Saving on electricity for heating
there's no hot water for shaving
so I boil the large electric kettle
in my bedroom for early morning tea
carry it in carefully to Helen
I still have after 70 years
the *peau d'orange* scar
on my right forearm from the scald
one London misty morning
before we left by car
up the A5 to Plas
past the water tank
the man with the hook
for a hand who serves petrol at Atherstone
tea at the Crown in Corwen
cold rice pudding
and stuffed owls
on the table in the dark corner
Daddy's aluminium metal shaving jug
with the black lid knob and handle
that flapped and made a noise
round bulbous pewter like
careful up the stairs
don't fall or slip on the carpet
Tannic acid jelly
the medication in 1938
the year that in Barking I first saw
Test cricket that summer on Uncle Will's
B and W huge console television
I've looked it up
against Australia
getting on for seven years old
and a bandage on my arm
in all the snaps on Rhosneigr beach
getting my first views on film
behind me of Tre Ceiri
dancing on the horizon.

KYFFIN

Now Kyffin is buried,
one more of my family slip out of the gallery.
Nain Plas being his mother's cousin
none of those two generations are now alive,
as dear Harold Owen Llynon
was used to say,
I knew his grandfather you know!
Another the old patient from Four Mile Bridge
who said he'd seen *Taid* drive
the blue *Overland to Dre,*
Holyhead on Market day,
the same old Grand Tourer that evacuees
William my brother and I
played in as it lay dying in the yard
by the duck pond,
stepping on the rusting running board
advancing and retarding
the imaginary ignition
with those shining aluminium levers
on the steering wheel.
What if these had really
worked in time travel
which way would we have wished to go?
There was no thought then apart from tea
or when we would see Daddy
back again from London;
we didn't know about the blitz.

THE STABLE

See a triangular shaft of dusty sunlight
painting pale yellow a square of tile,
on the floor of the stable,
the wooden stair a dark diagonal,
behind;
thinking of my mother.
Isn't that where she is perhaps,
lingering as a genie by the manger,
in an old forgotten bottle
of horse lineament from an age gone past
on a cob-webbed window ledge.
The air's so dry and danderous,
the clippers and combs are still here
from at least eighty years,
upstairs rust stained mattress ticking
where they slept, the stable lads,
and bits of harness.
So why not Mum,
remembering a romantic moment
in an old stable
before her sons came,
and had wives and complexes.

SUN WORSHIP

Summer comes,
The sleepy leaves swarm green,
As morning sunshine
Warms my children's limbs;
Our little sons,
Still sheltered from the world
Can bask at breakfast
In a prehistoric light,
Once worshipped on the solstice stone,
And spill their cornflakes
On the kitchen floor.

THE OLD BOAT

The old fisherman's boat
Floats gently in the July grass,
Her bows are pointing uphill
Where hen runs part
The tufted sea,
And settled low in the hay
At the stern of the butcher's shop
Bob Glandwr can see her still
Moored by his monkey puzzle tree.

ANGLESEY MIST

See where monotonous
Sea or mountain mist
Unlike the city,
Breathes security within enclosure
Steaming of familiar scenes,
And swirls,
The serial pleasures of the distant countryside
Sealed off.

RED WHARF BAY

In Memory of Burslem Griffiths

Boats hauled for winter ashore,
By the old warehouse
No more,
Three quarters of a yellow moon
Still,
Floating on the humid air
Where breathing lingers visibly,
A wreath of fading roses,
Sand and salty stillness
A strand.

NEWS ON THE HALF HOUR

".....and finally the teenager as yet unnamed is on a
ventilator his condition is said to be critical though stable
and now over to the sports desk.....",
he is balancing on the roof of his young experience,
tipping this way or that with air currents he could be said
to be on a knife edge,
with a strong gust he could slide on the wet school slates,
and as yet anonymous down into the dark sweet apple ink
and varnished school desk of his childhood,
the sequence of football first of course boxing tennis golf
and then to the weather,
prospects and travel will follow,
his heart is beating home and away and a draw is unlikely,
he was seeded well and relying on the pulse rate of the
US dollar which is falling,
pressure arrows pointing west can be seen in the sky
overcast overhead,
the market is oversubscribed all major routes are clear at
present and the vital centres,
report all channel crossings viable though variable in the east,
close family are advised to phone hourly,
our hot tip for today is still in the running,
his stable mate in the next bed has been scratched,
odds have recently shortened the weather is foul,
the pitch is waterlogged,
all routes are now blocked,
the stumps have been drawn..... that is the end of the news
here are the headlines again,
the as yet unnamed teenager.....

LEARNING THE GAELIC

For Nuala Ni Dhomhnaill

The phrase to learn today is
As dead as a herring.
Tha seamus bocchd cho marbh
Ni sgadan,
Neu sgodyn,
As we'd say here in Wales,
Being a little Latin fish
Caught from a *cwch* or a *llong*
Or a *navis longa.*
The Celts recognized a warship alright.
They are still to be seen in the lochs,
Or in Skye,
Heard on the bombing ranges
The tank traps of Eppynt,
Where the language is
As dead as a herring,
If you pardon the English.

THE VALENTINE CARD

Tonight you kissed me
Of your own accord
You did it
Directly and unconsciously
As a rare bird feeds
Seen close by
In the garden;
The room was not startled
As you bent down
Your lips thanked me
On my neck
Quietly.

GORSE BLOSSOM

Smiling yellow gorse blossom
sensually disinfects the lane
with a heavy mauve perfume.
Each spiny leaf a tiny spire,
furze pricking the blue sky
and me,
through my desire for Spring.

THE CWM PENNANT PICNIC

The river Dwyfor
Distillation from the mountain rain,
The moving surface film,
A pellicle of facets
To mirror angles of the sunlight
As it filters,
Split by branches overhead.
In places dark, dilate and swirling,
Where little flies will hover near the weeds,
The dilatation lets the water wander
Licking cattle trodden banks,
Whose hoof mark craters puddle.
Around a tree the narrows run
Between black boulders,
Dark green moss,
The water sluice injecting
A thrill into the pool,
Where we can dive and swim,
And be suspended.
As we bathe our minds will wander
In the amber water,
Revealing blood red pebbles
In the shallows,
And dark fish in the depths
Hiding under stones,
All senses probing out with the bank,
Dampened and disallowed
This afternoon.
Texture is exaggerated by the mood,
The rocks, the weeds, the grasses on the bank
Ask to be felt,
The current running a continuous thread
Of heightened tactile sensibility.
We bathed and dried on the warm turf of the meadow,

Hearing cars from up the fairy Cwm
Choke past at tea,
Moel Hebog had grown dark
The rain came heavily now and the
River heaved agog.

We all hopped in afraid of the *Tylwyth Teg.*
When it thundered we were already wet.
The rain sieved the flood,
Which rose and rising soon ran cold,
Even in the fiery lightning
Of the early evening storm.

GOOD FRIDAY

And now the mid morning
Sun, lights
me breaking fast,
to view the angle of the moon
subtended ten o'clock,
last night's.
How could the sky
darken this Friday
afternoon,
as I remembered as a child
the rabbit bounding,
pulls the sun
across the lawn.
But disaster threatens
outside the gate.

DIC

Dic in his yellow souwester
Before his monthly shot,
Sterile in wrinkled oilskins
Lest the midnight mushrooms steal his zest,
Bends his back to the oars
In the cold rain's curfew,
To row his blue and white boat at dawn off the grass,
Bows point through a glitzy foam of cow parsley,
Cleave brown rested waves of seeding dock plants
In the silver thaw of the morning garden,
The grey light and the roar of the surf from the bay,
Down to the running stream,
Where the white noise of water is playing over
The sand and salt pulse in his blood,
Washing about in the thwarts of his narrow skull,
Draw him off to the usually sheltered creek,
The Wig, the Viking bay.
He pulls past his crafted fishing fleet
On show on the mist wet wall of limestone,
Navigation lamps all lit,
Green to starboard!
Aground in heavy varnished timber,
Shrouds, lines, ready coiled
Nets he throws on to the grass,
Astarn!
I suppose he does it we say
To keep fit.
How sensible the split mind can be and greener
Than an exercise bike his habit of rowing,
But I know why he's pulling chanting to the bay.
On the chimney the sentinel gull sees all.
Pull away fiercely, gasping now,
To split the flood tide of his Autumn,
The rowlocks creaking to a climax.

Pull to escape
From the holidaymakers and their codified stare
Each night time in his best evening wear,
The gear, the Aran sweater,
The trousers with the seventies flare,
Where the lads sang hymns on Saturday nights
On the corner of the square.

Pull away wildly now
From the mildewed caravan,
The hammer and saw workshop,
Cradle of his model boats.

Oystercatchers pipe over his lime washed wall
While he pulls away,
From the old house by the cromlech,
Burial chamber of the early farmers,
Now his widowed sister is dead.
Pull away to sea!
On the chimney the sentinel gull sees all,
To the storm size fishing fleet,
To fish for mackerel.

Wait!
There's an easterly on to the lee shore,
Pull to sea!
Past the Wig and the island and slipway,
The old pulling lifeboats
Star of Sea One and Star of Sea Two,
The shiny new Lifeboat in orange and blue,
To the bay for the mackerel,
The mackerel are in.
Fresh mackerel!

Mecryll Fres!

COLLECTING THE EGGS

My books asleep
waiting for my morning call.
Roosting hens perched
lest I should wish to search
for the warm golden egg,
or a young pullet's egg for a feast
with a fellow poet.
Cackling and brooding
when a breath of inspiration
ruffles their feathers.
A few are stacked
like those of my flattened fathers
in a common grave unread,
fin de siècle, in the droppings.
Some free range from room to room,
circulate the house.
Others deep littered
stay sterile in the straw
unless favoured of the literary chanticleer,
to then produce their nuggets daily
in unlikely spots.
So my friend tread gently,
you tread on my breakfast.

CAPEL MORIAH

From the cold bedroom, short trousers and cold knees
to the warm bath of morning chapel,
best suit sitting in a varnished shuffle,
red carpet on the floor,
hot paint on the radiator.
Jim, our dog heard barking in the garden next door
through the grey opaque and closed windows
over the magnificent organ.

Mr Walter Hughes Chemy,
with an obviously rehearsed movement
pops another boiled sweet into his mouth,
looks at me across the aisle to pew 13,
crushes it with his back teeth
with a smile.
I'll flog you within an inch of your life boy,
With rubber tubing!
Repeat after me!
$2Pb3(NO3)2 = 2PbO + 4NO2 + O2$
He would say in the lab,
and we loved him.

Hated the Minister's expectant stare and crooked finger.
Are you coming up to say your verse William?
To the set fawr?
My baby brother's face went red.
He never came again to chapel.
Became a Professor of Adolescent Psychiatry,
Is buried in Scotland.

My mother's and father's coffins would stand
where we stood to recite,
to be received into the big chapel one day.
Nearby the carved varnished wood again,
black bows on the arms of the *pulpud,*
heavy Christmas flowers,
hot paint on the radiator.

MELIN EITHIN

Those silly damn hens
they won't go in out of the rain
even in high summer
when generations of nettles
and chickweed are luxuriant
spraying their pungent violet incense
of foxes in the grass.
I find old Morus sheltering
but cowering in the house
with faltering voice and handshake
fussed over by his calm wife.
He would have liked to have been hearty
but could never quite put it over
a failed romantic with a tremor in the cool kitchen.
What had I missed?
Disappointment in the family?
A secret concealed?
All I had discovered was the *melin eithin*.
Grit stone from the gorse mill in the fields
diagonal pocked grooves
painfully wrinkling the cowsheds gable forehead.
There was a certain coldness there always.
No gift of eggs but *leave the gate*
as I went
the only concession.

BUS TO MARKET

On Thursday I passed her standing by the road
Waiting for the bus
I have passed her like that many times
Her head scarf tied under her chin in the wartime fashion
Going to the market
Waiting in the shadows
Across the road where an old cottage is almost settled
In the undergrowth and nettles
By the field above the bog where the young lambs
Are kept or used to be kept

She was much thinner than I remember
Almost transparent
Maybe I had not noticed a tree
I recall her being slender
But she was plumper as a *Nain* and *Mam*
At times I have offered her a lift
Years ago now, knowing her family
Seeing her often with her back bent in the ditch
Reaching up to the hedge with an armful of umbelliferous white flowers
Hen blodau gwynion
Picking blackberries near the farmhouse
Quite an ordinary house
Under the sycamore trees

The son's farm now
Has new angular metal roofed sheds
Tractors machinery and implements
The old ones there rusting by the black plastic hay cocks
The house is still in shadow waiting by the roadside
The front door is new now double glazed
But that's from where I was always shown out of
Having called first at the kitchen at the side
The working door from the yard
Following in my father's footsteps his knock on the door
Calling out are there people in? *oes 'na bobl 'ma?*
Visiting the old man uncomfortable in the big bed

The children with a fever
Her once unhappy in the kitchen sweating pungently
Reluctant to go to hospital about something major

Now just passing
Still recognizing observing looking for signs
Seeing change wondering getting older
I looked after her mother once
When I first came to practice
Did I really see her there waiting for the bus
In the orange fallen leaves
The road leading to the blue hills of Lleyn
Or was it a memory shaped by longing
Waiting for the swifts on their sky pathway
Shrieking across the island?

THE BRINDLE DOG

A brindle dog
obeying all the rules
of light and of perspective
runs softly along
the path from my greatgrandmamma's
on the river Cefni
this morning from her house
where she had let him out
into my view
amongst the swerving swallows
those spermatozoa of Spring
the briefest touch of her hand on him
as he bounded out the door
and she withdrew
to brush her magenta hair
for her great grandson
watching from the balcony
of my house
with her eyes

LETTER TO IRIS MURDOCH

Good is the reality of which God is the dream.
- Iris Murdoch

It's so unfair that in a mere seven years
You went, and now I can never write
To thank you or even find an address.
You slipped into a gentle wilderness
Thorns from which you were never able to regain
The cultivated land of reason,
But to wander all of one long day and night
Without an apparent will to navigate.
You are my sundial, you were my compass,
I was able in those years to sail West
Holding the sun over my left shoulder
Warming my confidence, regaining faith
In self, creation and transcendent God,
The dream of which reality is Good.

Thanking Iris Murdoch for her book, Metaphysics as a
Guide to Morals, *published in 1992, I had a letter of thanks
from her husband Professor John Bailey of Oxford, several
years after her decease.*

BRYAN

Now the obscenity of the sickroom is over
It's quiet and simple in the chapel,
The morning sun warms the cream painted pews
From stage right, an occasional shuffle but
Nothing moves in this glass house.
Through the porch window above your flowers
Seeing a fly crawl on the pane
I calculate that one sheep grazing in the field behind
Is one hundred times as large
As the animals free on the field,
Without noticing the clouds blown by the north wind
Are constrained to graze and stay within the fence.
A gentle man, says one standing up, after a while,
Widely read and cultured, says another.
Two speak in English, one in Welsh,
Compare you with the *Just Centurion,*
I felt different seeing him, this was a man you could trust.
One lady stands up by a window on the left,
You and Julia and the Friends, she says,
Have honoured our little chapel today,
Founded I had noticed in eighteen twenty two.
Outside the toy churchyard
In a pocket handkerchief of ground
Acknowledges you as you pass with your family.
We all wait quietly for the Elders to shake hands.

In the village hall for the bunfight
I can see starlings strutting
About in the picture glass reflection on the wall,
Above the tea cups,
And see over my shoulder.
Nervously we laugh too loud perhaps,
Feel a disapproving glance.
You were already in the ground,
Your physical presence magicked away.
It is not a disrespectful sound,
Reminiscent of the fun that we had
When you judged the *Festival*
Poetry competition, in your old voice.

MOZART G MINOR QUARTET

A dry clapping of hands, a cough,
A music stand sits
Before the strings vibrate,
Sonority in the resonation of a bowing Rondo
Swaying in the rosinated warmth
Rhythmically,
As the instruments are moved around
By hands and knees,
The chins nodding,
The sounds shaking the heads and making sweat
Soak into the armpits of dresses
And suits and rot evening shirts
As they must have done two hundred years ago.
The questioning phrase,
The answers, too in cadence,
Repeated and changed,
The discourse brisk,
The dialogue rubbing strings aloud,
The air vibrates.

We shift our chairs uneasily on the polished floor,
It's like being quiet in church,
We're hushed,
The priests are cooking bread and wine,
It's corporeal,
Yet only sound,
The music must be somewhere in our heads,
Or our ears are just a medium
Open to a thought,
Yet, is it pleasure?
Is it being with you, and you, and you?
Your chair is squeaking, or your corset,
or is the fire too loud?
The traffic disturbing, the wind in the roof down here?
It's Mozart on the radio;
At least his thoughts,
The electric discharges in his brain
One snowy night in Leipzig
Which have come to life.

THE TANK, BENLLECH

Solid green glass water
high above my head,
in a quiet, dark, and choking place
unable to breathe,
not at all understanding,
then I was on the black marble
rocks again
by the Tank
in the summer sun,
and the sea flashing,
and the boys laughing
and fooling around as before,
I don't think that they had noticed anything.
But Henry had,
and seen my danger,
had dived in,
and saved me.
I must have been fourteen.
He perhaps eighteen or more,
like me he did Medicine,
was a flying Doctor in Australia,
had Alzeimers later
not even recognising his own brother Alun.
Died far too young.
But I am here now seventy five,
have dinner with his vet brother
retired like me
and we go swimming
together, with our wives

DROWNING IN MUSIC

For Jonathan Richards and his guitar.

Today I am relying on song.
Diving in from a grey morning,
Buoyant, swimming in music,
My tunes floating on a minim sea,
My breakfast recital
With tea contrapuntal,
Toast dripping in grace notes,
Celebrate in the street
Where we dance a mazurka,
Quaffing the wine of concerto ,
Swaying back in the rondo
Beneath a skyshine of quavers,
With Cecilia companion,
Drinking harmony for sustenance,
A cocktail for the dance.
The third century virgin
Never skipped in her life
So she said,
But today I shall teach her
That life is a song
And as cheap!

KEEP YOUR BLOODY CHIPS DEINIOLEN

Human thought is unable to acknowledge the reality of affliction. - Simone Weil

waking early with a fag
the dawn sun lighting the glistening hill tops
for a moment with expectation
the children speak in the choked voices
of their fathers and grandfathers
their language the everyday unshaven phrases
split down cleavage planes of harshness
blues greens purple shades of sputum
door steps shining in cold rain
bodies shaped out roughly
ready for the charge
lit by a kind word
waiting in the shelter of repartee
for the explosion
when emotions tumble down the cliff face
cigarette smoke disguises the dust
Duw it helps the morning cough man
they will tell me half joking
is laid by the low density fat diet
dignity of work
for only a bare wage packet
hand in pocket for either the linctus
or the magic bullet
can't afford both doc
to change the hue of the spit
put off the dread loss of pulse in the foot
cadw dy blydi chips!
a luxury to be able to say that
up in the hills

MACLEOD AND I

Macleod my car talks as I drive
We have been such good friends for years
Driver and car
Not just the squeaks and the rattles that jar
Which like those of my joints
Are signs of his age
But the faraway voice
In the fascia the cage
Where a car's soul lives
There is more than one voice
Like the roar of the engine
When I change gear roughly
Whine if I push it too hard
He will sing also alto if I let him so do so
His aerials whistle
Raising spirits on my magic island
Opera sometimes and jazz for the bard
And he talks back at me
Whenever I shout or I cry and scream or bellow at night
Mindlessly round the bends on the wet road winding
Our father who is at the rudder getting us right
Into the calmer sea and into the still waters
Of the dual carriageway
Descending to the many reflections of
Bethesda at sunset
We thrill together approaching the Menai Straits
I can hold the mountains and the jewels of Caernarfon
In the palm of my right hand
Revolving slowly off the wheel
Lift the land and the houses up to see underneath where
The gas and power lines are dangling
Drains dripping as I rotate the land of Arfon at will
We discuss it together
Hooked down by gravity
White upturned farmers' faces stare in fear
Condescending smiles on the farmers' wives
Faces their laces snap
As the hand picks up traces on the land
Like cables trailing crazy furrows
On red and virgin fields below
Llyn slowly unfurls a large sod for the fire
And the ground cries
For the old Saints as we swerve
Don't I drive the front axle
Would you say so Macleod
In a beautiful gentle goidelic curve
Urged by centripetal forces
Neither you nor I can grasp?

MEDICAL HOUSING POINTING
IN DOLGELLAU

On the coach road just as I thought
I am doing well
I have got away!
reflecting on the textural excellence of the car radio,
Braint, the Elizabethan farmhouse on my right said
Hallo cousin!
Comfortable squat Tudor chimneys settled in a wavy roof of small tiles,
gave a slow smile, and a family voice sent a warm shiver of continuity
before I left the island,
my land, of my tribe, to the 4th to the 7th to the 9th kinship.
The mood kept with me
all the way south,
and over the rock to Meirionydd,
crossing commotal boundaries, rivers and abbey lands.

Of the applications for re-housing in the Office,
many were from England.
No points had been given under the scheme
for local qualification.
The common phrase was *personal preference to relocate.*
An old house or a friendly hill
may have nodded on holiday, but there could be *no medical advantage*
for me to take up,
the rules being what they were.
I should have liked to smooth her ageing brow
with an old cottage on the ground floor,
a certificate of belonging to loosen their arthritis,
and a pedigree to ease his angina.
But they will stay trapped now
in the familiar streets of bleak irritation,
High Street shopping and shots of hospital wards on TV
to illustrate cutbacks,
it's what they are used to, after all.
Perhaps someone can escape from Milton Keynes
after a glance in the secret
microfiche in the black market book
of desirable terrace houses
in villages with 6th century churches like Penmachno?
Did I dream that?
What dreams do they have?
How many points can I give
for a broken heart?
They could be distant cousins.

FEARFUL SILENCE

Fearful silence in a tranquil place.
My blood courses far too loudly,
sat so close.
The puppeteer
gently tugs my strings,
I have to stand,
she's in control.
I turn my head towards her,
a little jerk to blink my eyes,
I come as if alive.
My mouth grins
and blows a wooden kiss.
That was yesterday.
and since then
the brief touch of her hand
still pulls me.
The smile in her eyes
works me.

GLADIATORS

It was Paris
the *Arena de la Lutece*
the first and only time
I have ever seen two women fight

Sitting down for the open air jazz,
the vibrato of Bechet's soprano sax
soared over the St Germain rooftops
into the blue evening sky.

On the next seat to Martin and I
they started tearing each other's hair
then simultaneously both
pulling off their high heeled shoes
they fought like hot cats screaming
until removed by the gendarmes.

I shook Sidney Bechet's hand
calling him *Mon President*
as he was honorary President
that year of the London Jazz club,
held his sax in the interval

The sky was indigo
and I had forgotten the fight
until now hearing this year
that on these magenta summer nights
they still use stilettos
to fight at Flint with
an eye for an eye.

LA GIOCONDA

Three weeks ago in Menai Bridge
a rainy languid lunchtime lingering
in the Deli by the window
espresso poring over the crossword
glancing past arranged Italian pastas
the virgin olive oil and cheeses
out to where a car had stopped
in traffic for a while
piled high as Roman *pili palas*
mountain bikes strapped up upon the boot
their askew wheels so slowly turning backwards
the lady passenger smiling
gently at the shop and me
I gasped it was herself !
La Gioconda!
No other No it couldn't be
Her wry slow and curious stare
as I imbibed her face her hair
I would have known her anywhere!
She turned full forwards and *momento*
I was the very first to ever see
the *profile* of the *Mona Lisa!*
She turned again to me in that soft light
framed between two panes of glass
and *SMILED !*

The next day was April Fools
then I might have understood
why on *bella una giornata*
my vision had been so intimate
she truly saw me
sitting having lunch!
and as I watched
Leonardo and his bold model
on holiday drove off the tyke!
I would have never guessed
he rode a bike
as well!

GWERCLAS

Home visits from a locum Dr

Give me a four storeyed house
where the timbers show,
the old family gone
but their spirit grow
all over the lush green ragged garden,
under the high brick wall.

The stately Dee flows
from right to left,
we can see the white church
on the other side,
and the ford when
the mountain tide of rain is low.

There is a peace of mind here, inside
the wooden walls of the later hall,
below, strong coffee, welcome,
and home made cakes,
served on the oak table
the size of the cool slate slabs
of the gegin floor.

The space above the children's room
is wonderful,
and like an upturned boat.
I thought it might have been
old Humphrey's room,
whose grandson Hugh
married the daughter of Thomas Yale,
of the family who founded that College,
and was King Charles's captain
in the Civil War.
He slept here, where
I heard an owl,
that night when I visited,
under a new moon.

The walls are safe and comforting,
but beg for candle light and a lamp,
on the wooden stairs from the governess's room
where the children tramp
and is now the loo.

The moon light shone
on the cobbles
growing there
on the inside court,
through the doorway high enough
for a man and a horse,
a traveller, to walk in slow to the oldest part.
It's a garden still, and might have been
where the famous herbs were grown,
by Mali, Rebekka, and Gwenhwyfer,
Ales, Francesca, Magdalen and
Dorothy one and two, and use to flavour their stew.

The attic creaks in November winds,
the plaster and lath between the joists is dry
protected against the January snow.

Love jumps across entailments
and lines of a family tree,
the happy shrieks of Gus
and the children playing ball
on the green grassy mound,
the *werk of the name,* above the Dee,
weave through the crucks
and beams of the stable roof,
the oldest part still above the ground,
they found when they pulled down the older house
and extended more.
They made smart red bricks in the field nearby,
and put up the crest so proudly above the door,
Two boars' and three Englishman's heads
facing South, over two sundials on the lawn,
to their sheepwalks and lands of Owain Glyndwr.

The entrance Hall is bare but for remains
of coloured Georgian swags on the walls,
the woodwork straight from the fashionable
London pattern books of the local architect.
Upstairs, the rooms are stitched through
with sounds from the floor below
the composite whole, red clay, and oak
and the children's play, have built a timeless ark
to carry a family safely through
the floods of an alien age.

FLINT CASTLE

From the first train
the red tint of sunrise
put flesh on the castle at Flint,
high baked brick chimneys aimed
Victorian streets at the heap.
What a size, what windows,
what a view of the Dee.
Placid the cirrus sky,
The Keep placed by the Cooling Tower
stayed, from miles down the line,
serene majesty and power
lost in a Barbican of industry,
whilst in the dark I passed again
the sandstone molecules held still.

PAIR WALKING

Walking walking walking still
slowly as one together
in rhythm with his brother
which the elder
neither a winner
easily a pair
whatever the weather
they climb and descend
the vale and trails
of Pentraeth
past Tyn Coed and Merddyn Gwyn
slightly bending
turning in conversation
to the others shoulder
perhaps he the older
indivisible as one body
moving with a rocking motion
they are so similar
in their new rain wear.

Today we're worried aware
of having seen neither
taking the air
measuring the footpath
or in the Square
sitting with Nancy
and the other seniors
where are they ?
we wonder gently.

WALKING IN PAIRS

Girls have such
different faces from us
do they know?
How is it they don't?
their smooth skin
chiselled lips and presumptuous
noses
pampered cheek bones
excite us
fascinate by their contrast.
Unconsciously they walk
in pairs
tossing their sweet hay smelling hair,
occasionally floating
a violet glance,
turning your heart over
from a flickered eye.
One face stamped North Wales
cast Iberian,
her friend's moulded
in alabaster,
stained by her auburn hair,
heedless of my stare,
as I passed,
just a man in a car passing
and looking.

WHAT'S ON THE PICTURES ?

What's on the pictures?
The Majestic
Down at the Regal
Over the Plaza
Up at the Odeon
No that was last week at the Hippodrome
No not our Rialto
Their Adelphi
I do miss the old Olympia
The Arcadia was our local
And the Luxor out east
And the Metropole for dances too
And the Carlton
The Savoy was good though wasn't it
We used to go to the Corinthian of a Sunday
Or the Everyman
Foreign films you know French and the like
Miss the old News theatres the Bijou the Gem
The Wedgewood remember the Grafton
Plenty of cartoons and serials
But the Theatre Organ was the thing at the Royal
Tommy Dando coming up out of the floor
Playing *Keep Your Sunny Side Up!*
And everyone singing
And the Showgirls the Royalettes
Hide The Side That Gets Blue!
What about those flea pits
The Stella the Green the City in Bangor
With double seats in the back row
Your Mam used to pay in jam jars you said
She said in Francis Street Dublin
Bet she had no ice cream half time then
Better than sherbet
I hate sherbet

Come on we'll be late
For the Roxy
Oh I thought we were going to the Empire
It's showing at the Palace too
Or is that closed now
That's Bingo
What about that new place in the Junction
Be Like Two Fried Eggs
Keep Your Sunny Side Up!

HOME FROM THE PLAZA

Returning from the pictures
the car threw itself like a wave at the shore of the house,
a burst of laughter smacked at the walls and choked the bricks.
The bastions stood.
Splashed anecdote and snatches of joke
dashed themselves at the windows.
Their mother's laugh heard higher pitched amidst the spray
collecting in runnels and filling the valleys between the rocks
as the laughter swirled in pools and ran through the front door
in burst of merriment ebullient
bursting in globular bubbles
ripples dissipating
on the floor of the kitchen.
It was a good film
I had kept my feet dry upstairs.
Good old Indiana Jones.
And then the last programme of the night.

THE RAPE OF THE STAIR

Craigle set up on the wooded hill above the Bay,
has views of distant Great Orme's Head
and yet the hills of Clwyd,
my home was once a warehouse for the bird manure
of the Cinchas islands in the far Pacific,
saved by our intrepid locals sailing round the Horn.
So thus we have three storeys
reached by narrow stairways.
Aye! And there's the rub!
As they say in rude Americee.
A trapdoor in the dining room to the master bedroom,
another to the guest room, up above,
where the winch hung out above the drive.
A horse and wagon from up the beach,
full Guano loaded, when the Brig dried out,
drove through to where our dining table sits.
My legs are tired,
my spine is too
narrowed so they say,
to give me problems
climbing stairs,
and thus the purpose
of this lay.
It was mooted that we have a 'gin,
to hoist me up the way.
Three companies came to fight their cause
Oh! How I rue the day!
The Abbey won, at least they said
"there is no problem, we'll come next week,"
and so it was they did.
Two burly men, a son and father too,
"You will get used to it" they smiled,
when leaving teatime,
having filled our stairway
with aluminium tracks, chairs and footrests
into which for me to squeeze.

My wife, she screamed!
My stairs have gone,
to say nothing of that carpet that we laid.
Oh! Woe is me!
They've raped the stair.
What is now there to be done?

So now for days with family,
good kind friends, and experts in the trade,
we kept good counsel.
Remove the newels and the banister,
seemed the majority answer.
And what instead?
And Oh! My head!
It's spinning with the dread.

I've made my decision,
there will be no incision!
At last a smile!
No more measuring up
For yet awhile!
Remove this Bauble!
This is my final say,
I shall walk up
While I'm able!

In many ways a fair description of our house.
The exercise is good for me, but Helen still has
the burden of carrying washing etc upstairs.
A new carpet is in the offing.

THE IRISH WASHERWOMAN

Picking me up deftly
By
My shoulders,
She squeezed my throat,
My two arms she forced behind my back
And twisted up.
Turning me on my tummy
I was flattened by the weight of her hand.
There!
That's the way to iron a shirt
In thirty seconds!
She announced triumphantly,
Buttoning my fly.

THE OLD CONVENT

It's dark here in corners
nuns gone there must be holy dust
of bread and wine intense
molecules of incense oscillating
within an arc of the swinging censer
aimed by the man priest
defying hells angels
amongst the virgin novices
and yet the stones remain cold
North of England marble at the altar
does not speak of such things
the walls have lost the stations of the Cross

hidden by boards of recent exhibitions
no flagged floor was ever laid
except in dreams
worn smooth by years of cold medieval feet
in rough leather sandals
at the old Abbey
with relics in the crypt
money in the bank of Cayman
those drowsy hooded figures walking
down
     in
       single file
          on a flight of stairs within the wall
habits hardly making the candles flicker
their energy would be spiritually contained
now encapsulated in an Arts Centre

PORTRAIT OF JANE WELSH CARLYLE

Your portrait of 1855
Is so tantalising
Like your smile to someone.
Your complexion and cheeks interest me
You are in black of course,
Or is it crimson your dress
To hide your fidelity?

I have a knowing look,
Have I not?
My smiling chin
Hand cupped and
Propped on my skinny elbow, itself
Resting on a book on the table,
Where the alabaster baby lies.

It is to stop me giggling
At what I said to the photographer.
An albumen print,
I ask you!
A sign of the times,

Whatever next?
I am sweating dreadfully under my arms
I have only just come in from feeding
My hens.

I shall tell Thomas
When he is back from his ride.
He just sits there in his top coat for a portrait
For his artist,
Holding his walking stick,
An event in history I suppose.
Perhaps he thinks he is Frederick the Great,
It is very funny indeed.

How long do I have to stay
Like this Mr Wilkes?
You are right my dress is crimson.
I am not telling him but I am

Gey ill to live with today
And Thomas is no better.

Do you really want me to lean
My chin on my elbow,
Or just pretend?
Why do you want the book?
Is my arm not long enough?
My humerus I mean!
There I made you laugh again.
That will spoil it for you,
I hope not, after all your preparation.

I wish my Thomas were here.
He is so lively once more,
After a book is finished,
And he is never grumpy when he is out
Riding with his friends.
Perhaps I can amuse him with the story
Of the portrait when he gets back!
Or I could write him a letter!

HUNTING THE WREN

The wood grained
wren
flew on
wings the colour
of our family gramophone
projecting
childhood's master's voice
and darker wood than that
covering my wise
father's arthritic knuckles
twisting now
as the flesh decomposes
by its own chemical action

HELA'R DRYW

Y dryw
Lliw graen pren
A'i hynt uwchben
Ar adenydd unlliw
A gramaffon ein teulu gynt
Gan adleisio
Llais meistr ein plentyndod
Ac yna'r pren o dwyllach gwawr
Yn cuddio migyrnau arthritig fy nhad doeth,
A ddirdyna'n awr
A datgymalu
Yn y chwalu terfynol..

Translation by Glyndwr Thomas

ASLEEP

Asleep this afternoon
A slip of vision
Saw a series of ellipses
Kissing lips so Grecian,
Careless eclipses caressing and crossing,
To sweep up in a graceful curve,
To sip and pout,
Yet utter not a word,
A servant of the thought,
The will, the voice,
To open and impart,
To breathe,
To carry waves of modulated sound,
But smile a little even sleep,
In simile or silent love.
The breadth of your eyelid
Lies between
The breath of love, and
Birth of new life.
An angle subtended
By the eye
In the viewer of the lid.
Grey shadow enamelled,
Rather though,
Dilator, owner, flicker,
Late shutter and opener
Of my Iliad,
Lashed and blinkered,
Lulled to sleep by the poppy
Of the morrow.
In that idyllic wink
We bred
Our children.

NEW LIPS

Lips such gentle inclines
raised red rounded delicate and fissured hills
patterned for tongue's glossal slopes
to ski down slowly
from a patent palate
saliva slipping glissando
on warm flesh and blood
or in a kiss
a magnet for eyefuls
dilating eagerly for love
fascinated by the swiftly changing symmetry
lower and upper forming bows
as the surgeon's revealing fingers heal
exposing fresh new shoots of pasture
the soft skin of emotion
swelling smiling suckling
to foster speech
puckering pursing to an O
to allow sweet smelling breath to flow
for now and for a lifetime.

*Thoughts after attending a Charity function at Judith Moss's
house for 'The Smile Train' Cleft Palate repair operation for
Young people in the Third World. As a Registrar in Dublin I
had assisted in such operative surgery.*

INTERNATIONAL SMILES

Your smiling sunburned face,
a physical representation
of your Valentine's Day phone call
from Portugal last year.
Your smile that I had remembered for eight years
in Ireland
and drew you home to Wales.
Your smile,
the flame that still always burns for us.

RENOIR'S GARDEN
St Paul de Vence

There was peace within the askew frame
the olive farm on an island
between three lanes,
the ground smelling of cut hay
and dry earth.
We ate Renoir's cherries
refreshed ourselves from his garden tap
as we sat on the bank
in the shimmer of midday.
His life and family portraits
shut up in that sultry house,
and the olive mill was broken.
But we sat with him in his garden
a few days before the bulldozers
rearranged the frame.

TŶ NEWYDD, WINTER 1945

There were no leaves yet
In that sepia photograph in the little Museum.
The coffin had been borne from the house.
Horse and wagon waited under the eight windows
where a dormer would follow much later,
looking out on his final resting place and listening
to Afon Dwyfor chattering away as usual,
shaded by the trees, with
momentous news to tell of Tadau's death.
Taid the Welsh wizard
at the close of his second Great War.
There is always feeling in this old house.
Ghosts gather on landings,
blurred colours and figures
at the red garden gate.
An air of centuries exists around the kitchen,
the central sensual core,
language students barefoot
at night on the tiled floor.
Those medieval builders
chose wisely on a well known site,
a hall dwelling of their forefathers,
unknown to us,
by river water,
a safe distance from the coast,
words settling over centuries
on traditional homeland and green pasture,
a space to think and write.

*Earl Lloyd George's Funeral, leaving Tŷ Newydd,
Llanystumdwy, Cricieth. National Writers' Centre for Wales,
Translator's House and Taliesin Trust.*

LON PENMYNYDD

Travelling homeward after midnight,
the road bisects the Gemini,
four and half degrees apart,
loosened from a string of beads
into the brown peat sky,
the car surfing the ecliptic
on a pavement of May blossom,
tyres squealing on the sepals of the stars.
From Gwydion's palace garden,
River Dance of the Milky Way.
Eridanus is no straighter
than this old road
of peasants and of kings,
crossing Braint for Bran, and Ceint and Cefni,
Caradog and Crigyll for Branwen.
No river rushing
with more momentum than I do
to the pansy purple sea;
but a tired man driving home ,
along a warm dark road,
where younger men were waking to the gibbet,
for unrecorded crimes.
Owen Tudor Loves Katherine de Valois
Is scribbled on the petrol station wall,
Elin took her young life so quickly,
Swift's stage coach runs down the hill,
haunt of pink Silene,
to Nuala Ni Dhomhnaill's surprise;
past the big houses that count,
Castell, Dragon and the Plas,
Pwll Tregarnedd my Hippocrene
for watering gallows' horses,
only noted like those of Achilles,
ready for a last journey
to unmarked graves of felons

unnamed, joining the patients of
Hippocrates and the good thief
on The Cross.
I pass by where Borrow strides
so eager for his pint and chop
bardic talk and silence and a pint of sherry.
Well! Gentle reader he says,
All bills must be paid,
It's better to pay them with a smile!
With no ale
in his starlight dreamtime
equating Methodism and oats;
though he and Wesley
eat in the same Bull's Head,
half a century apart.
No gilded horns but bleeding
in each other's fields.
They fade as I turn into Bulkeley Square.
No flowery faced owl here to woo,
but the Thursday market stalls greet me.
Goodihoo!
As their rallentando
by the river
wakes the dawn,.
I gasp in excitement
to hear a voice in the wind,
time exhaling into my face.
And so she keeps on blowing
that daisy breath
becomes no more a roar
than a corncrake's complaint
over the sea marsh and Cob Malltraeth,
drying the stalks of the rushes,
rustling the backs
of the yellow sycamore leaves,
straining to recall the beginning of Spring.

SIWAN'S FAREWELL

To chance and the Prince's quiet satisfaction
that February the weather was mild
for the short journey.
Siwan
would not be waving
her fair hand and arm raised in salute,
her oxter angle open
allowing a falling mantle
to reveal her bare defiant shoulder.
Llanfaes beckoned
The Royal Barge,
the Ferryman having had more than his usual fourpence,
slid from Abergwyngregyn over Lafan
as the head of the Orme abaft
gnawed the line of the horizon,
margin even of yesterday's dominion.
The ebb lapped,
today her realm suddenly expanded
as she left Llywelyn Fawr
her primum mobile
and his conquered boundaries,
for her empyrean,
fulmars wheeled above
with their exaggerated dihedral.
Y Tywysoges Siwan,
Princess Joan, moved slowly further
to her an outer sphere,
from the flat shore,
from William Brewys unmanacled en fin
buried in the hillside bracken.
She could see it all now mid stream,
the fat round Tower and the Gatehouse
the hills, the Falls behind
sheltering Garth Celyn,
in the Hafod the cattle at milking,
the Gardens and home.
Joan would lie for seven centuries
on the island

under the floral carved stone,
in the Friary and then wilderness.

The priests meet her
as they will for her grandson's wife
Eleanor de Montfort
dying in childbirth of Gwenllian.

Bare voices chant
intermittent halfnotes
to greet her,
Siwan
wife mother and daughter of Princes.

HENFFORDD ABERGWYNGREGIN

But was it all in vain?
We had travelled so slowly
with Gwenhwyfer
progressing home from Conwy,
harness muffled ever moving rhythms,
the creaking cart behind bearing
the still warm body of the master,
the soft *gwynt Awst*,
our faces to Cochwillan,
his bloody head nestled in our lap.

The mist had cleared,
on our right Penmon,
Ynys Seiriol lay below
abaft across y Fenai,
the wild raspberries an ornament
along the lane.
The quiet voice
echoing in our ears
four hundred years again,
or was it yesterday
straining for tranquillity
from the expressway.

PANDY BENLLECH (The Fulling Miller's Tale)

We had but scarce English
when we ran the Pandy
water was my life.
The stream ran below Tyn Iolyn
there I farmed
hard by the burial place of the old people.
Our land ran down to the sea
where the boats beached in Benllech
by the Wig where the brig carried our woollen cloth
with millstones dug from out the Bwlch
shipped to the Norwe
ours to the Lerpwl and Briste.
I had no shares in the boats.
My cows were strong then
their horns gently knocking
against the wooden stalls for milking
when I could manage the rent,
the horse neighing sometimes on a moonlit night
as I listened in the dark to the wind,
gauged the rain and how much fell
above Tynygongl fields to fill the pool
to turn the Wheel for the paddles
to beat the wool.
Then fine weather later stretching out the cloth
on the green slope above the house,
and the smell of piss
even at night was everywhere.

The friendly stream
still runs by the gable of our home,
except in winter when it floods.
The little voices drowned then
by the deep excited chorus
of a thousand rivulets smacking their lips.

Rhed y ffrwd garedig eto gyda thalcen noeth y ty

PILGRIMAGE

I see the Rivals always with surprise,
Mirage, a faint image,
Summer blue and faithful.
They have always been there for me,
Never trivial, familiar, a friend.
Day time Orion to find and wave to
When since on the sands a smudge seen on the strand
Sun burned calamined and bandaged,
I saw hills dance in a rocky pool,
Playful, Triple, and Eyeful sans pareil,
An open window to yr Eifl,
My blue double ewe,
Indigo infilled Cassiopea.
I love the way their zig zag peaks appear to graze the mist
With their tricuspid nibble,
Skim rake the cloud veil, escallop the sky,
Waltz in triple time,
Lift wild skirts of sloe berries,
Tuck up the pink hem of the morning.
Three sisters point arthritic fingers at the men of Leinster.
Ireland's that way they whisper.
Today I am driving to Pwllheli,
Leaning across the arm of the land,
The level playing field of the sea's bedstead
Allowing the mountain to raise her knees
For a morning stretch under a green tatterdemalion of fields,
The Devil's shawl of Salem,
Coverlet of clouds lifting slowly for a yawn
To let the early morning sword blade of the Eastern sun
Kiss the nipple line of Lleyn,
Bending to suckle Clynnog on the shore
Where holy Beuno paddles endlessly
Waking an unkyndness of ravens on Tre Ceiri.
Every pererindod is a journey
Between meninges,
The two sides of the mind adjacent.
But there is one desire to satisfy
And one for penury
To travel as a pilgrim and a penitent.

BLUEBOTTLE

Bugger it!
A bluebottle in my morning tea.
I heard its buzzing swoop,
a Junkers dive then slap,
hitting my crossword or my head
so I checked quickly with my hand.
I had not noticed,
neither had the ploughman and his team in my garden,
Icarus fly screaming down from the sky,
nor had the yacht in Red Wharf Bay
on their quiet passage
seen his terrible flight that day.
Four drops of tea slopped
on the bedside table
splashed from his re-entry,
his?
so he was a male fly?
There he was anyway, all legs
and mouth parts and his funereal
chitin body in the drink.
The overnight milk had been fresh
and the tea with one sugar sweet.
But the fly landing had mistaken
light from the window
as runway not ground zero.
Out of bed I flushed the cup away
afraid now that I would suffer
guilt,
of slaughtering innocence
however unconsciously.
I am still sorry,
and tea, for a while is tainted.

MORNING EPIPHANY

Oil slick at the pump
my stick slips
I rotate
fall
on to hard grey granite
rectangular cobbles
the garage forecourt
I can't rise again
or move

two tall angelic men
lift me up
or lower me down?
it feels cold enough
and final

Helen looks so warm
her limbs and torso inviting
making tea
in her white
brushed cotton nightgown
in my room
this morning
how can I be dreaming?

MY HEAD

I feel my head
bone felt
hair short
it is so small
and hard a nut
to contain all
that makes me remember,
squeeze out speech,
tears, love, scream, scowl
and run towards or away
from daily life,
and as for dreams,
why,
if that is where they come from,
I scarcely believe!

WAITING ROOM

No one waiting for you Doc!
But he had got up this morning
to prepare to come.
Will you see another one?
He doesn't know that he's an extra.
In the night he had woken
as he often did now, in a cold sweat.
Was it those crows at the window?
He had gone to bed with the salve
of the Surgery in the morning,
on sufferance though, his wife is insistent.
The water's hot, cariad, she says,
seeing his thin frame in the huge bath,
an obscene baby,

just flicking and dabbing water
in the white enamel sarcophagus.
The pain persistent,
the toilet calling, even whilst shaving.
He had cut his chin,
a piece of the Daily Post did the trick,
All the appointments are taken I'm afraid Mr Jones!
Mr Jones?
Who me,
Wil Ty Pen?
Yes, but you can wait if you like.
He wondered where the toilet was,
found it, in two languages,
why had all these young girls
so many kids running around.
An elderly lady nodded slightly,
but she was too grand, and wore a hat.
Where I sat waiting,
I wanted to go home, only one more,
I rang the bell.
Only one waiting now!
squeaked reception,
for the last judgement.
He knocked quietly and hesitated,
I knew your father,
he smiled.
Come in and sit down,
I said, in the warm room.

Biographical Note

I was born in Ilford Essex, now Greater London. In 1939 my mother, brother and I were evacuated to my father's home, Plas Llechylched, the family farm, on Ynys Mon. Later we all moved to Llangefni, on the island, where my father continued in practice as a Family Doctor.
I studied medicine at the Royal College of Surgeons in Ireland, of Dublin, graduating in 1958.
For 30 years I practiced as a Family Doctor in Benllech, on the island, and for a further 15 years as a *locum tenens* after the progression of my disabling arthritis.
I had written poems since a schoolboy at Rydal, and later submitted to a small number of magazines and journals.
This is my only large selection to go for publication.
For 12 years, until 2011, I was on the Board of The Taliesin Trust, Tŷ Newydd, the National Writers' Centre for Wales.
I have been directing the Literary Society of the Canolfan Ucheldre Centre, Holyhead, for a number of years.

Dr O C PARRY-JONES